Ladybird Readers

I Love Food!

To access the audio and digital versions
of this book:

1 Go to **www.ladybirdeducation.co.uk**
2 Click "Unlock book"
3 Enter the code below

FpgQ8B2SaQ

Notes to teachers, parents, and carers

The ***Ladybird Readers*** Beginner level helps young language learners to become familiar with key conversational phrases in English. The language introduced has clear real-life applications, giving children the tools to hold their first conversations in English.

This book focuses on the statement "I love", and introduces food-related vocabulary in English.

There are some activities to do in this book. They will help children practice these skills:

 Speaking  Listening* 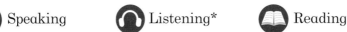 Reading

*To complete these activities, listen to the audio downloads available at **www.ladybirdeducation.co.uk**

Series Editor: Sorrel Pitts
Chants by Sorrel Pitts

LADYBIRD BOOKS

UK | USA | Canada | Ireland | Australia
India | New Zealand | South Africa

Ladybird Books is part of the Penguin Random House group of companies
whose addresses can be found at global.penguinrandomhouse.com.
www.penguin.co.uk   www.puffin.co.uk   www.ladybird.co.uk

Penguin
Random House
UK

Text inspired by *Today Is Monday* by Eric Carle, first published in Great Britain by Hamish Hamilton, 1994
This version first published by Ladybird Books 2024
001

Printed in China

The authorized representative in the EEA is Penguin Random House Ireland, Morrison Chambers, 32 Nassau Street, Dublin D02 YH68

A CIP catalogue record for this book is available from the British Library

ISBN: 978–0–241–58787–4

All correspondence to:
Ladybird Books
Penguin Random House Children's
One Embassy Gardens, 8 Viaduct Gardens, London SW11 7BW

MIX
Paper | Supporting
responsible forestry
FSC® C018179

Ladybird Readers

I Love Food!

Inspired by
Today Is Monday
by Eric Carle

Do you like beans?
I love beans!

5

Do you like pasta?
I love pasta!

Do you like soup?
I love soup!

Do you like fish?
I love fish!

Do you like ice cream?
I love ice cream!

Your turn!

1 **Talk with a friend.**

Do you like beans?

Yes, I do / No, I do not.

Do you like pasta?

Yes, I do / No, I do not.

2 Listen and read. Match. 🎧 📖

1 I love pasta!

2 I love soup!

3 I love fish!

4 I love ice cream!

3 Read and clap!

"Hello, hello! Do you like food?"
"Yes, I love beans and pasta!
I love food!"

"Hello, hello! Do you like food?"
"Yes, I love soup and fish!
I love food!"

"Hello, hello! Do you like food?"
"Yes, I love fish and ice cream!
I love, love, love, love food!"